I0617299

All the Best

SONGS FOR YOUTH

The Greatest Choruses,
Praise Songs,
and Contemporary Artist Favorites

Compiled by Dennis Allen

Arranged by Dennis Allen, Steven V. Taylor, and Tom Fettke

SONGBOOK

Lillenas PUBLISHING COMPANY

KANSAS CITY, MO 64141

1
Shine

Steve Taylor

Peter Furler

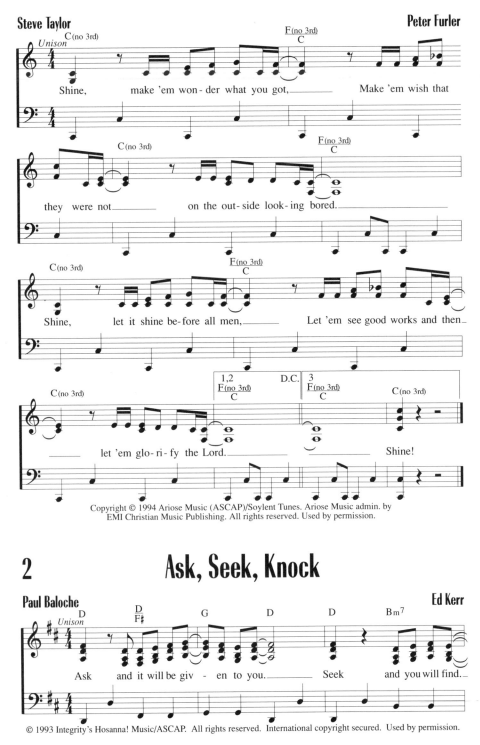

Shine, make 'em won-der what you got,_____ Make 'em wish that

they were not_____ on the out-side look-ing bored._____

Shine, let it shine be-fore all men,_____ Let 'em see good works and then_

let 'em glo-ri-fy the Lord._____ Shine!

2
Ask, Seek, Knock

Paul Baloche

Ed Kerr

Ask and it will be giv - en to you._____ Seek and you will find._

3

Willing Heart

Words & Music by
David E. Bell

Lord, give me a will - ing heart, _____ Lord, give me a brand _____ new start. _____ Cre - ate in me _____ a love that's real, _____ Give me a will - ing heart. _____ Lord, give me a will - ing heart, _____ Lord, give me a brand _____ new start. _____ Cre - ate in me _____ a love _____

I Pledge Allegiance to the Lamb   4

Words & Music by
Ray Boltz

Big House

Words & Music by
Mark Stuart, Barry Blair,
Will McGinniss & Bob Herdman

5

1. I don't know where you lay your head_____ or where you call your home._____
2. I don't know if you got some shel - ter or say a place to hide._____
3. All I know is a big ole house_____ with rooms for ev - ery- one._____

___ I don't_ know where you eat your meals_____ or
___ I don't_ know if you live with friends_____ in
___ All I know is___ lots of land_____ where

shade.
had.
me?

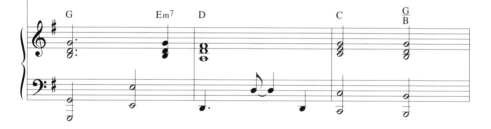

2,3 CHORUS

Come and go with me____ to my

Fa - ther's house;____ Come and go with me____

Change My Heart, O God

Words & Music by
Eddie Espinosa

I'm Not Ashamed

Peter Furler & Steve Taylor

Peter Furler

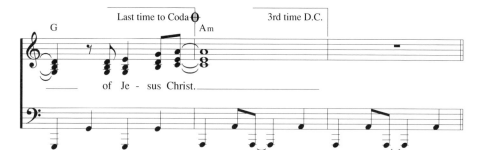

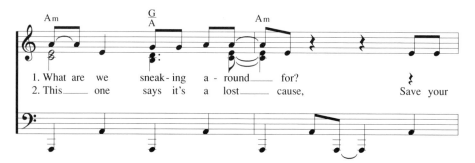

Lord, I Lift Your Name on High

Words & Music by
Rick Founds

Lord, I lift Your name on high. Lord, I love to sing Your prais-es. I'm so glad You're in my life. I'm so glad You came to save us. You came from heav-en to earth to show the way, From the earth to the cross, my debt to pay. From the cross to the grave, from the grave to the sky,

Lord, I lift Your name on high! ___ high! ___ high! ___

Here Is My Heart

9

Words & Music by
Jonathan Wolfe

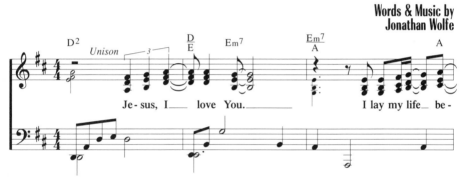

Je-sus, I ___ love You. ___ I lay my life ___ be-

- fore You. ___ I want to ___ know You. ___

Here is my ___ heart. ___ heart. ___

Stuff of Heaven

Words & Music by
Jeffrey B. Scott

1. I used to like to___ dream

2. We mea-sure our suc - cess - es___

that I'd be rich be-yond com - pare.

by all the things we've got.

I'd nev - er have a wor - ry_____ in the world,

Who- ev - er has the most toys wins_____ in the end,

E7   A7   A7sus

_____ I'd nev - er have a care._____

_____ least that's what we've been taught. ___

A7   E7   E7sus

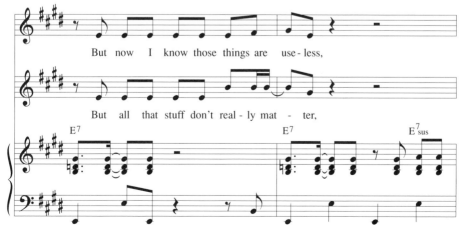

But now I know those things are use - less,

But all that stuff don't real - ly mat - ter,

E7   E7   E7sus

caus-ing wor-ry and__ pain.__

it's just rust and de-cay,__

The one true wealth I've got to fol-low

and when we get to heav-en

is the pow'r of Je-sus' name.

we can't keep 'em an-y-way.__

CHORUS %

See fame and glo - ry don't count much in the Fa -

ther's eyes, or seek-ing ob-jects made_____ of_____ gold._____

_____ The on - ly things that mat - ter are

faith, hope,___ and love. The stuff of heav - en will_____ nev - er grow old.___

B   C#m   A (no 3rd)

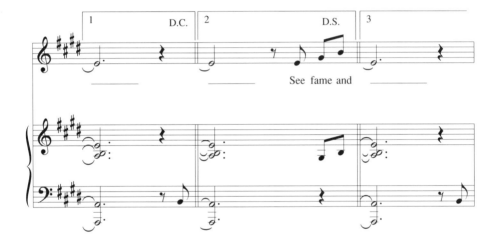

1   D.C.   2   D.S.   3

See fame and___

E7   E7sus   E7

Seek First

Words & Music by
Amy Grant & Wes King

Seek first the king-dom of heav-en and all

shall be add-ed. Seek first the king-dom of heav-en

and all shall be add-ed.

They say we need mon-ey and pow-er They say
Don't they know our Friend in high pla-ces? Noth-ing

there's no God up a-bove.
can be strong-er than love.

12 God Is Gonna Finish Just What He Started

Words & Music by
Morris Chapman

God is gon - na fin - ish just___ what He start - ed
E - ven though the wa - ters got___ to be part - ed.
Lift up your heads;___ don't___ be bro - ken - heart - ed. God___
___ is gon - na fin - ish what He start - ed in you.___
start - ed in you.___   He who be - gan___ a good work___

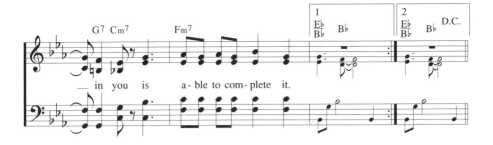

I Love You, Lord

13

Words & Music by
Laurie Klein

I love You, Lord, and I lift my voice
to wor - ship You. O my soul, re - joice!
Take joy, my King, in what You hear;
may it be a sweet, sweet sound in Your ear.

14   I Will Lift High

Words & Music by
Dan Whittemore

I will lift high____ the Lord God at all times. I will sing His praise the rest of my years. I sought the Lord__ and He gra-cious-ly an-swered. He took a-way__ from me my great-est fear. He took a-way__ from me my great-est fear.____ For the eye of the Lord__ is up-on __ me; His ear is at-ten-tive to my ev-ery cry. His

We Are Standing

15

unknown
arr. by Dennis Allen

*2nd time, sing "We are"

16 You Are My All in All

Words & Music by
Dennis Jernigan

1. You are my strength when I— am weak, You are the trea-sure that— I
2. Tak-ing my sin, my cross,— my shame. Ris-ing a-gain, I bless— Your

seek. You are my all——— in all.
name. You are my all——— in all.

Seek-ing You as a pre-cious jewel, Lord, to give up, I'd be— a
When I fall down, You pick— me up. When I am dry, You fill— my

fool. You are my all——— in all.
cup. You are my all——— in all.

CHORUS
Opt. 3 part

Je - sus, Lamb of God, wor - thy is Your

name. wor - thy is Your name.

Pharaoh, Pharaoh

17

Words & Music by
Tony Sbrano

CHORUS
Unison

Pha-raoh, Pha-raoh, oh, ba - by, let my peo-ple go. *Uh!*

Yeah, yeah, yeah, yeah, I said: Pha-raoh, Pha-raoh, oh, ba - by, let my

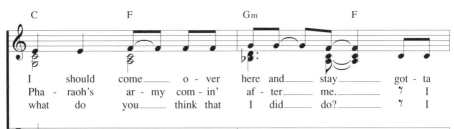

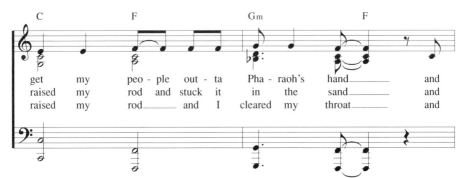

18   Be Bold, Be Strong

Words & Music by
Morris Chapman

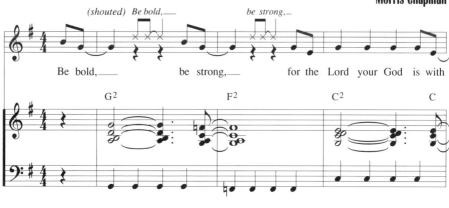

(shouted) Be bold,—   be strong,—

Be bold,—   be strong,—   for the Lord your God is with

G2   F2   C2   C

Be bold,—   be strong,—

— you.   Be bold,—   be strong,—   for the

D   G2   F2

Lord your God is with— you.   I am not a- fraid;—

C2   C   D   C   D   Em   D

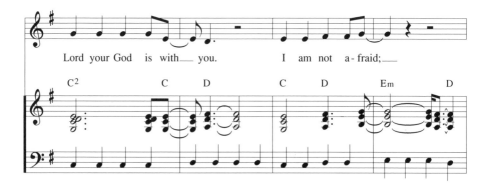

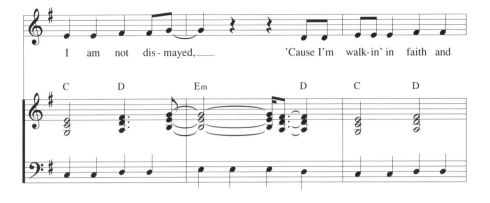

I am not dis-mayed,___ 'Cause I'm walk-in' in faith and

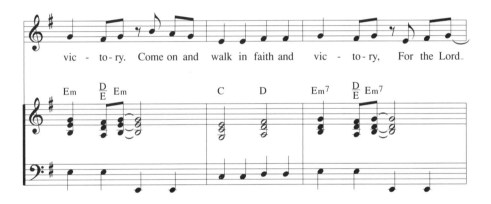

vic - to - ry. Come on and walk in faith and vic - to - ry, For the Lord___

___ your God is with_____ you.___

19 Jesus, You Alone Are Worthy

with
Worship You in Spirit

*"Jesus, You Alone Are Worthy" (Jennifer Randolph)

**"Worship You in Spirit" (Danny Chambers)

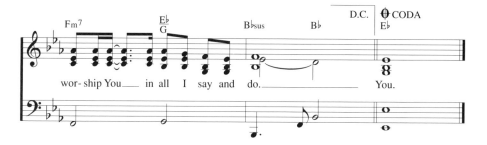

O Lord, My Rock

20

Words & Music by
Cathy Jeffers Risse

21 I Believe

Wes & Fran King

Wes King

1. I believe in six days and a
2. I believe I - sa - iah was a pro-phet of

rest.
old.

God is good, I do con -
The Lamb was slain just as He fore -

Words and Music by
Mark Altrogge

23   If God Is for Us

Words & Music by
Eddie DeGarmo
& Dana Key

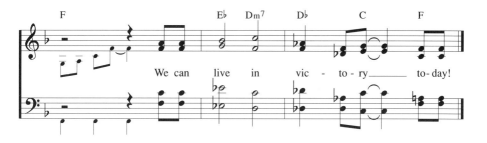

We can live in vic - to - ry ____ to - day!

Let Me Love You 24

Ken Bible

Steven V. Taylor

My Fa - ther, let ____ me love ____ You, love ____ You,

love ____ You From a heart ____ that's o - pen ____ and

lis - t'ning for ____ Your voice. ____ Let me love You, ____ tru - ly

love You, ____ sim - ply love You, ____ lov - ing ____ Lord.

25 Celebrate Jesus

Words & Music by
Gary Oliver

Cel - e - brate Je - sus, cel - e - brate,

Cel - e - brate Je - sus, cel -

- e - brate. Cel - e -

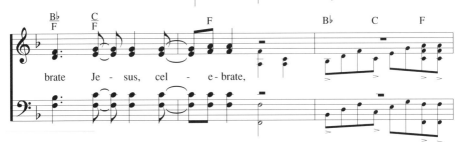

brate Je - sus, cel - e - brate,

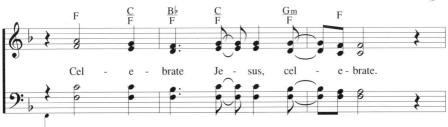

Cel - e - brate Je - sus, cel - e - brate.

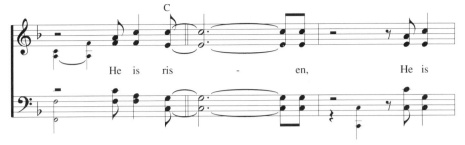

He is ris - en, He is

ris - en, and He lives_____ for- ev- er- more;__

_____ He is ris - en, He is

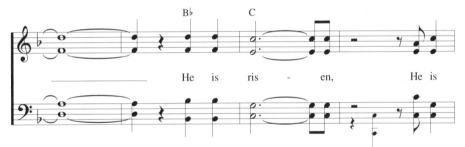

ris - en, come on and cel - e- brate__

the res- ur- rec - tion of__ our Lord._____

Jesus Is a River of Love

26

Words & Music by
Dallas Holm

27
Trust in the Lord

Adapt. from Proverbs 3:5-6

Dennis & Nan Allen

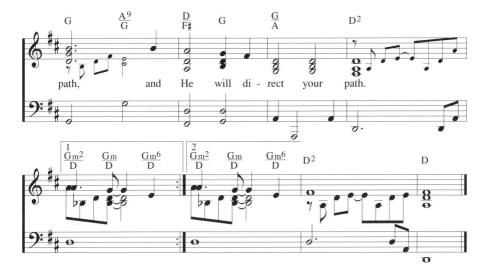

path, and He will di - rect your path.

No Fear

Words & Music by
David Bell

28

There is no fear in Je - sus Christ; By His

grace we're made new. It's the cross that re - minds

— me, That in Him— no fear.

*optional - echo each phrase

29 Not Ashamed

Words & Music by
Danny Chambers

CHORUS

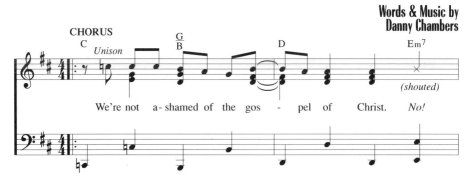

We're not a-shamed of the gos - pel of Christ. *No!* *(shouted)*

His Word is pow - er to save us.

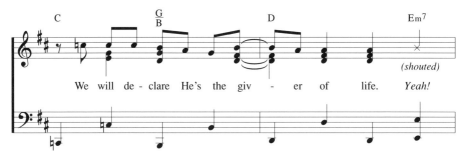

We will de - clare He's the giv - er of life. *Yeah!* *(shouted)*

last time to Coda

For - ev - er we'll sing His prais - es.

All That I Need

(My Only Hope)

Word
John Paul ...

31 Stand Up and Shout if You Love My Jesus

unknown
arr. by Dennis Allen

(loud) 1,2,4. Stand up and shout__ if you love my Je- sus. *Yeah!*
(soft) 3. Sit down and whis-per if you love my Je- sus. *Yeah!*

Stand up and shout__ if you love my Lord. *Yeah!*
Sit down and whis-per if you love my Lord. *Yeah!* I want to know, yes,

Open Our Eyes 32

Words & Music by
Bob Cull

1. O - pen our eyes, Lord,_____ we want to see Je - sus;_____
2. O - pen our ears, Lord,_____ and help us to lis - ten;

_____ To reach out and_ touch Him,_____ and say that we love
{ O - pen our_ eyes,

Him._____ Lord,_____ we want to see Je - sus._____

33 Carry the Light

Words & Music by
Twila Paris

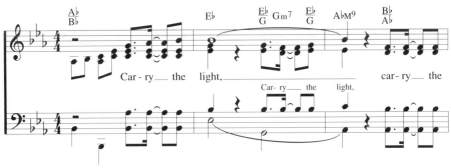

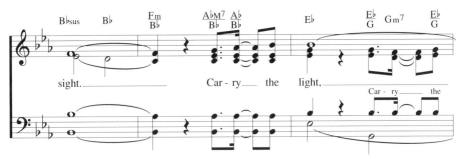

Be the One

34

Words & Music by
Al Denson, Don Koch
& Dave Clark

there is no___ more night.   In the name of Je - sus Christ,___

___ car - ry___ the light.   light.___   Car - ry___ the

light,   the   light.   Car - ry___ the   light.___

1. Will you be   the one_____   to an-swer to___ His
2. Yes, I'll be   the one_____   to an-swer to___ His

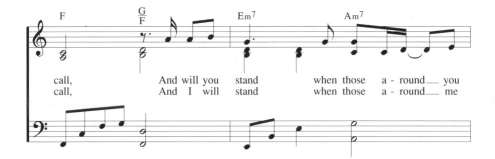

call, And will you stand when those a - round____ you
call, And I will stand when those a - round____ me

fall? Will you be the one_____ to take His light in - to a dark - ened
fall. Yes, I'll be the one_____ to take His light in - to a dark - ened

world?_____ Tell me, will you be____ the one?
world._____ Oh,____ yes, I'll be____ the one.

one. Yes, I'll be the one_ one.

Awesome God

35

**Words & Music by
Rich Mullins**

Our God is an awe-some God; He reigns from heav-en a-bove with wis-dom, pow'r, and love. Our God is an awe-some God! God! Our God is an awe-some God! Our God is an awe-some God! Our God is an awe-some God!

36   The Kingdom of Our God Has Come

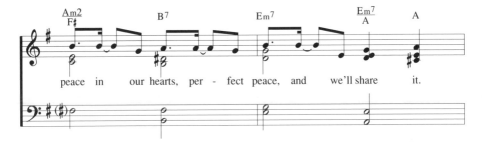

peace in our hearts, per - fect peace, and we'll share it.

Trou - bles may come, but in Him we will bear it.

Joy is in Je - sus! We have to de - clare: The

king - dom of God has come! O life and

Yes, the king - dom of our God has come!

Step by Step

37

Words & Music by
Beaker

O God, You are my God, and I will ev-er praise You. You. I will seek You in the morn - ing, and I will learn to walk in Your way; And step by step You'll lead me, and I will fol-low You all of my days. days. And step by step You'll lead me, and I will fol-low You all of my days.

38   I Want to Be a History Maker

Words & Music by
Graham Kendrick

Let Me See

39

Words & Music by
David Bell

earth as it is in heav - en. earth as it is in

heav - en. I want to be a his-t'ry mak-er.

O-pen my eyes, let me see. O-pen my ears,

let me hear. O-pen my heart, let me love

You, Je - sus. I love You.

40   Jesus Is the Rock

Words & Music by
Tony Congi

41 God Will Make a Way

Words & Music by
Don Moen

God will make a way where there seems to be no way.
He works in ways we can not see,
He will make a way for me. He will be my guide,
hold me close-ly to His side, With
love and strength for each new day, He will make a way,

He will make a way.

God Still Moves

42

Words & Music by
Chris Machen

God still moves, God still moves, In the hearts of His peo-ple He still moves. He does not sleep nor does He slum - ber. God still moves, God still moves.

43   Jesus Is Lord of the Way I Feel

Words & Music by
Don Francisco

Praise the Lord, Hal - le - lu, I don't care____ what the de - vil's gon - na do! The Word in faith____ is my sword and shield; Je - sus is the Lord of the way I feel. I say I feel. O clap de hands, stomp de feet, Spread the love of Je - sus with ev - ery - one you meet! O clap de hands,

stomp de feet, Spread a lit-tle love a-round! I say now

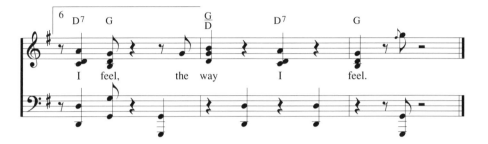

I feel, the way I feel.

Friends 44

Words & Music by
Michael W. Smith & Deborah D. Smith

1. Pack - ing up the dreams God plant-ed
2. With the faith and love God's giv - en,

In the fer - tile soil of you;
Spring - ing from the hope we know,

Can't be-lieve___ the hopes___ He's grant-ed Means a
We will pray___ the joy___ you'll live in

chap-ter in___ your life___ is through.___
Is the strength that now___ you show.___ But we'll keep you close

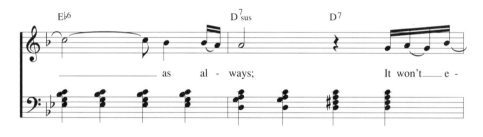

___ as al-ways; It won't___ e-

-ven seem___ you've gone,___ 'Cause our___

hearts in big and small ways Will

keep the love that keeps us strong. And

CHORUS

friends are friends for-ev - er If the Lord's the Lord of them. And a

friend will not say "nev - er" 'Cause the wel - come will not end, Tho' it's

hard to let you go, In the Fa - ther's hands we know That a

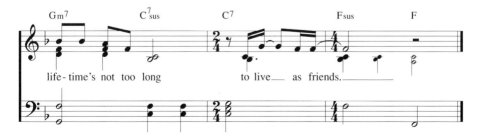

life - time's not too long to live as friends.

45 Let My Life Be the Praise

Words & Music by
Dennis & Nan Allen

Let my life be the praise that rais- es You, Lord. Let my life be the praise; Be glo-ri-fied in all that I do, As a dai-ly re-flec-tion of Your god-ly per-fec-tion. Let my life be the praise,

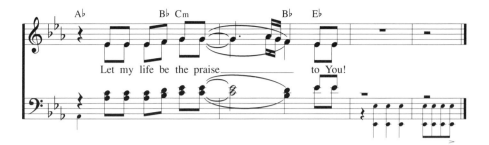

Let my life be the praise_____ to You!

For the Sake of the Call   46

Words & Music by
Steven Curtis Chapman

We will___ a - ban-don___ it all   for the   sake of___ the call.___

No oth-er   rea-son___ at   all–   for the   sake of___ the call.___

Whol-ly___ de-vot-ed   to   live and___ to   die for the sake of___ the

call._____   call._____   call._____

47 From the Rising of the Sun

unknown
arr. by Steven V. Taylor

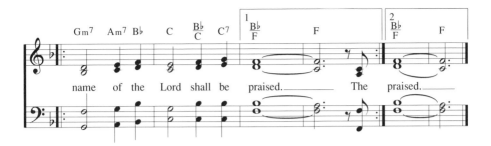

name of the Lord shall be praised. The praised.

What a Mighty God We Serve   48

unknown
arr. by Keith Phillips

What a might - y God we serve.

What a might - y God we serve.

An - gels bow be - fore Him, heav - en and earth a - dore Him;

What a might - y God we serve.

49 Victory Chant

Words & Music by
Joseph Vogels

Lord, Be Glorified 50

Words & Music by
Bob Kilpatrick

51 I Believe in Jesus

Words & Music by
Danny Chambers, Jillian Chambers & Trent Austin

1. When the fi - res rage and the heat is on
2. When the pres - sure's on and friends are few

I won't bow down I'm stand - in' strong! When dark - ness falls,
I'll risk it all and speak the truth. When the loft - y looks

my voice will rise a - gainst the tide of com - pro - mise.
of i - dols fall by faith in God I'll be walk - in' tall.

I'll take it to the streets a - round the world, a song of love

*Option: girls down one octave until Chorus

_____ and _____ free - dom. _____ Pro - claim the creed _____ He lives _____ in _____ me!

CHORUS

I be - lieve in Je - sus. _____

I be - lieve _____ that He died for me. I be - lieve _____ that He set me free!

I be - lieve in Je - sus. _____ I be - lieve _____ that He rose a - gain

for the heart _____ of ev - 'ry man. for the heart _____ of ev - er - y man. _____

52 I Waited Patiently

Words & Music by
Danny Chambers

I wait-ed pa - tient-ly for the Lord___ and He in-clined to me and heard___ my cry.___ He al - so brought me up out of a hor - ri - ble pit, out of___ the mir - y clay,___ and set my feet___ up-on a rock, ___ and es-tab - lished___ my___ steps.___ He has put

a new song___ in my mouth.___ Praise___ to our God!___

Ma- ny will see___ it and fear

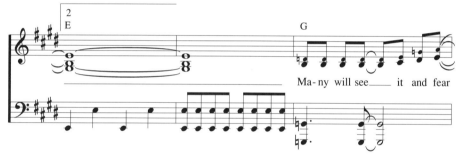

and will trust___ in the Lord.___

Ma - ny will see___ it and fear___ and will trust in the Lord.___

53

Sing unto the Lord

Words & Music by
Russell Lowe

Sing un-to the Lord,— sing to Him a new— song.

Sing un-to the Lord,— sing to Him a new— song.

Sing un-to the Lord,— sing to Him a new— song.

Sing un - to the Lord,___ sing to Him___ a new___

song. Sing un - to the Lord a new___ song,___ play

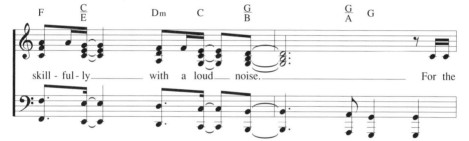

skill - ful - ly___ with a loud___ noise.___ For the

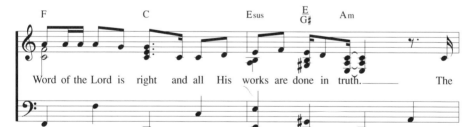

Word of the Lord is right and all His works are done in truth.___ The

earth is full of the good - ness of the Lord.___ song.

Whatever He Wants

54

Words & Music by
David E. Bell & Rod Padgett

1. I don't have the strength_____ to make it through the day.
2. The fu-ture's un-clear_____ and ev-ery-thing's hard to see._____

So, I close my eyes, all I can do is pray.
I'm fac-ing the fear of what is in-side of me._____

Lord, help me to stand,_____ give me the words_ to say,
Lord, I call on You,_____ You see me through_ each day.

so they can see You_____ as I go on my way.
You give me the strength_____ as I go on my way.

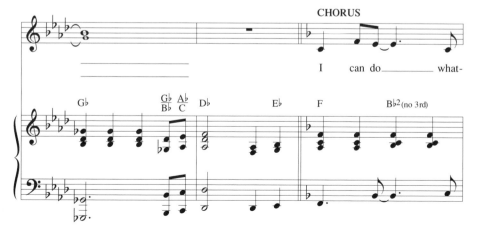

CHORUS

I can do_____ what-

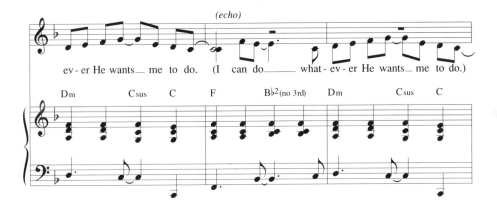

ev - er He wants— me to do. (I can do—— what - ev - er He wants— me to do.)

I can do—— what - ev - er He wants— me to do. (I can do

—— what - ev - er He wants— me to do.) Filled with— His pow -

er, He'll see__ us through,__

stand-ing to-geth-er, We'll do what He wants__ us to do.__

Praise Him, Raise Him 55

Words & Music by
Dan Carson

56 Pass It On

Words & Music by
Kurt Kaiser

1. It on - ly takes a spark to get a fire
2. What a won - drous time is spring when all the trees are
3. I wish for you my friend this hap - pi - ness that

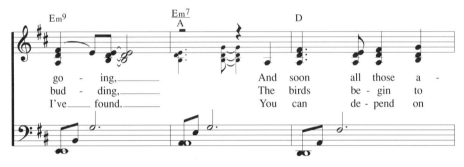

go - ing, And soon all those a -
bud - ding, The birds be - gin to
I've found. You can de - pend on

round can warm up in its glow - ing.
sing, the flow - ers start their bloom - ing.
Him, it mat - ters not where you're bound.

That's how it is with God's love,
That's how it is with God's love,
I'll shout it from the moun - tain top,

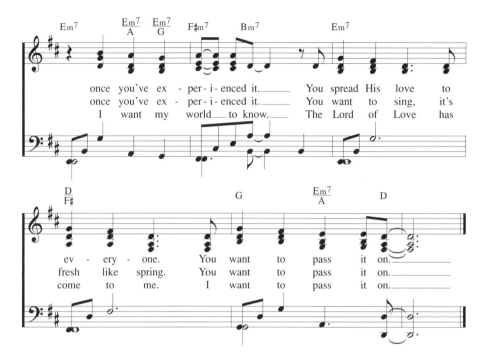

once you've ex - per - i - enced it.___ You spread His love to
once you've ex - per - i - enced it.___ You want to sing, it's
I want my world__ to know.___ The Lord of Love has

ev - ery - one. You want to pass it on.___
fresh like spring. You want to pass it on.___
come to me. I want to pass it on.___

I Give All to You   57

Words & Music by
Larnelle Harris

I give all my *serv-ice to You.___ I give all my serv-ice to You.___ No

mat-ter the cost___ or what oth-ers do,___ I give all my serv-ice to You.

*Additional verses: problems, family, future, worship.

58

I Am Somebody

Words & Music by
Al Holley

Only You

59

Ken Bible

Steven V. Taylor

60 Lean on Me

Words & Music by
Bill Withers

CHORUS

Lean on me___ when you're not strong,___ and I'll be your friend;

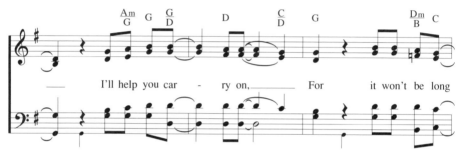

___ I'll help you car - ry on,___ For it won't be long

___ till I'm gon - na need___ some - bod - y to lean___ on.

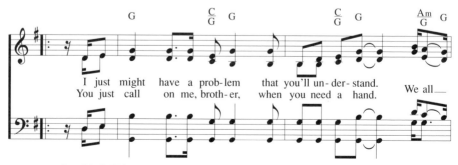

I just might have a prob - lem that you'll un - der - stand.
You just call on me, broth - er, when you need a hand. We all___

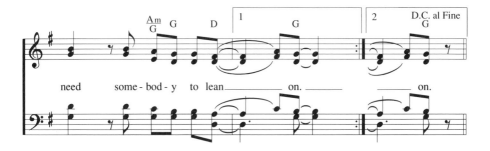

need some-bod-y to lean____ on.____ ____ on.

You're the Reason We Sing 61

Words & Music by
Dan Carson

Je - sus,____ we come____ to wor - ship____ your name.

____ You a-lone____ are wor - thy, we

crown you King____ of Kings.____ Ho - ly, ho - ly, ho -

- ly, let the prais - es ring.____

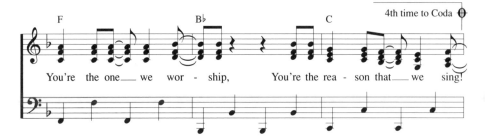

You're the one___ we wor - ship, You're the rea - son that___ we sing!

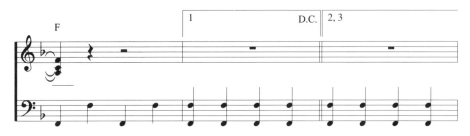

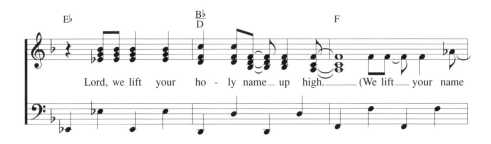

Lord, we lift your ho - ly name___ up high.___ (We lift___ your name

___ up high.)___ Lord, we wel - come You,___ our spe - cial guest.

___ (You are___ our spe - cial guest.)___ Lord, we're here to

sing our praise to You. (We sing our praise to You.)

You're the one, the rea-son that we sing!

D.C. (both times) CODA

You're the one we wor-

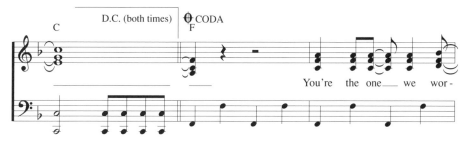

- ship, You're the rea - son that we

sing!

62 Sing, Shout, Clap

Words & Music by
Billy Funk

This is the day_____ of cel - e - bra-

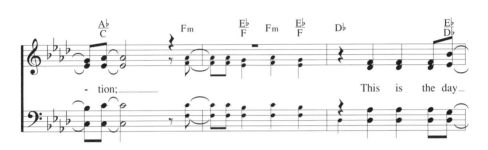

- tion; This is the day_

_____ to re - joice!_____

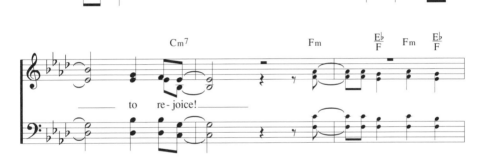

The Lord,_ our God, is our_ De - liv - er - er,_

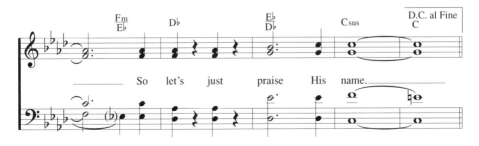

_____ So let's just praise His name._____

63 I Humble Myself Before You

Words & Music by
Bruce Wickersheim

Lyrics:

CHORUS

I hum-ble my-self be-fore You, fall-ing down at Your feet; I hum-ble my-self be-fore the King of Kings. And, wor-ship-ping at Your foot-stool, I of-fer my heart of praise; In hum-ble-ness, Lord, I mag-ni-fy Your name. You are the Ho-ly One; You are the Righ-teous Judge,

Cre - a - tor of all life, and Sus - tain - er of my

soul.___ hum - ble - ness, Lord, I mag - ni - fy Your name.

God's Not Dead 64

unknown
arr. by Dennis Allen

God's not dead, *No!* He is a-live!___ God's not dead, *No!*

He is a-live!___ God's not dead, *No!* He is a-live!___ I can

feel Him in my hands; God is a - live!

feel Him in my soul; feel Him in my eyes; feel Him in my

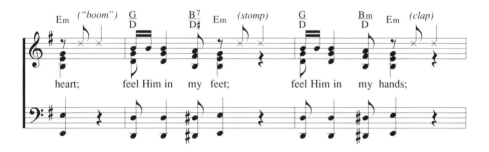

heart; feel Him in my feet; feel Him in my hands;

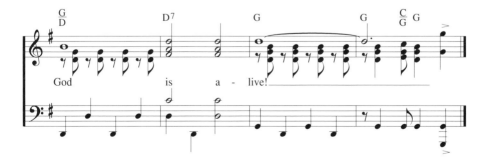

God is a - live!

65 His Strength Is Perfect

Words & Music by
Steven Curtis Chapman
& Jerry Salley

I can do all things thro' Christ who gives me strength, But some - times I won - der what He can do thro' me. No great suc - cess to show, no glo - ry on my own, Yet in my

CHORUS

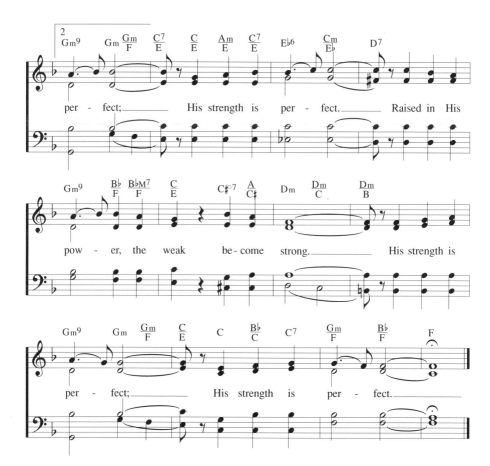

per - fect;_____ His strength is per - fect._____ Raised in His

pow - er, the weak be - come strong._____ His strength is

per - fect;_____ His strength is per - fect._____

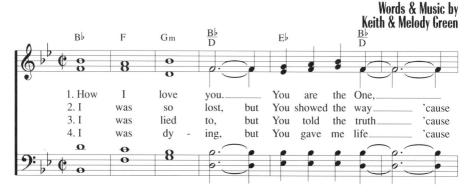

66

You Are the One!

**Words & Music by
Keith & Melody Green**

1. How I love you._____ You are the One,
2. I was so lost, but You showed the way_____ 'cause
3. I was lied to, but You told the truth_____ 'cause
4. I was dy - ing, but You gave me life_____ 'cause

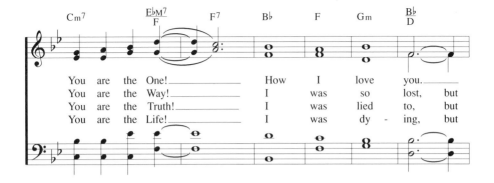

You are the One!   How   I   love   you.
You are the Way!   I   was   so   lost,   but
You are the Truth!   I   was   lied   to,   but
You are the Life!   I   was   dy - ing,   but

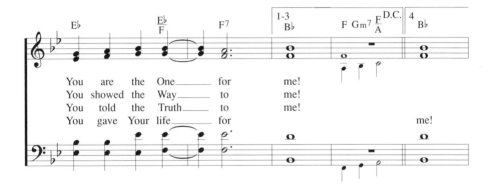

You are the One   for   me!
You showed the Way   to   me!
You told the Truth   to   me!
You gave Your life   for   me!

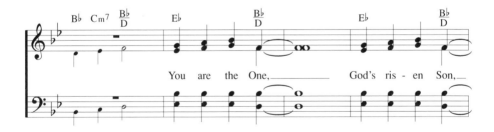

You are the One,   God's ris - en Son,

You are the One   for   me.

67
Shine Out the Light

Words & Music by
Dave Clark, Al Denson
& Don Koch

Shine out the light, _____ shine _____ out the light; _____

Shine out the light _____ to the world. _____ Like a

can-dle in _____ the dark-ness burn-ing thro' the night, _____ We've got to

shine out the light___ to the world. ___

Hosanna, You're the King 68

Words & Music by
David Bell

Ho - san - na, You're the King, ___ We

Echo

Ho - san - na, You're the King, ___

more,⌣⌣⌣⌣⌣⌣⌣⌣⌣ for - ev - er -

for - ev - er - more,

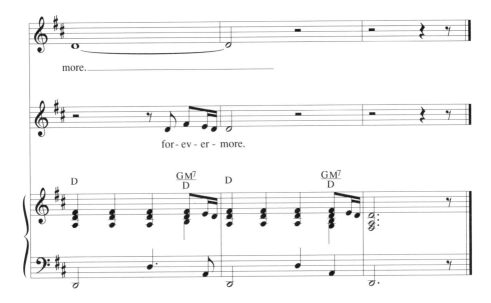

more.⌣⌣⌣⌣⌣⌣⌣⌣

for - ev - er - more.

I've Got Something to Say

Words & Music by
David Harris, Jeff Gunn
& Brian Tankersley

Hey now, peo-ple, I've got some-thing to say,___ sing-in',

"God's not dead.___ *No!* His chil-dren aren't a-shamed."___

Hey now, peo-ple, we're not just here to play.___

Stand up, shout it! There's pow'r in Je-sus' name!___

Hey now, peo-ple, I've got some-thing to say.___

Spring Up, O Well

70

unknown
arr. by Steven V. Taylor

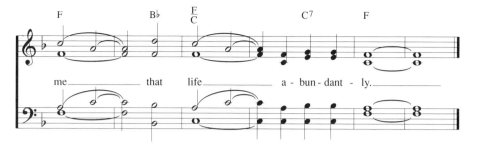

me____ that life____ a - bun - dant - ly.____

Shine, Jesus, Shine 71

Words & Music by
Graham Kendrick

Shine, Je - sus, shine;____ fill this land with the Fa - ther's glo - ry.

Blaze, Spir - it, blaze;____ set our hearts on fire.____

Flow, riv - er, flow;____ flood the na - tions with grace and mer - cy.

Send forth Your Word,____ Lord, and let there be light.

72

The Blood of Jesus

O the Blood of Jesus
Nothing but the Blood
There Is Power in the Blood

arr. by Dennis Allen

*"O the Blood of Jesus" (unknown)

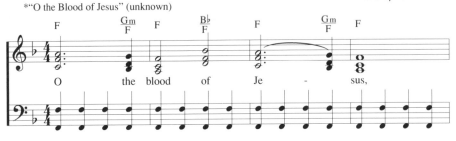

O the blood of Je - sus,

O the blood of Je - sus,

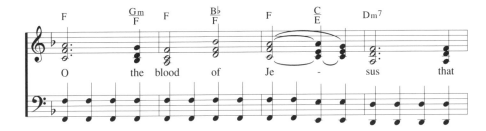

O the blood of Je - sus that

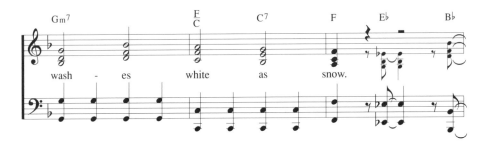

wash - es white as snow.

*"Nothing but the Blood" (Robert Lowry)

What can wash a - way my

sin? Noth - ing but the blood of

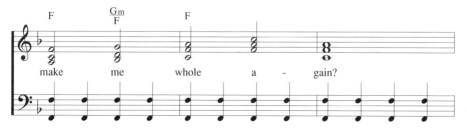

Je - sus. What can

make me whole a - gain?

*"There Is Power in the Blood" (Lewis Jones)

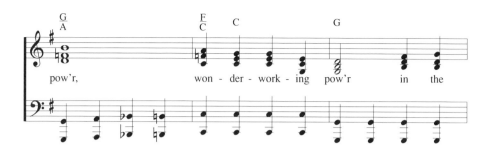

pow'r, won - der - work - ing pow'r in the

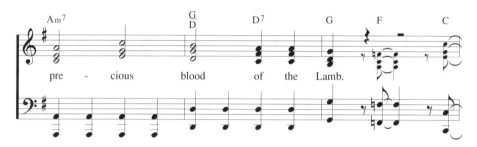

pre - cious blood of the Lamb.

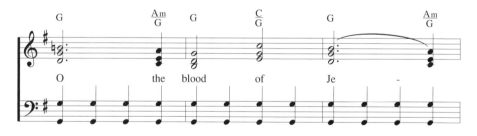

O the blood of Je -

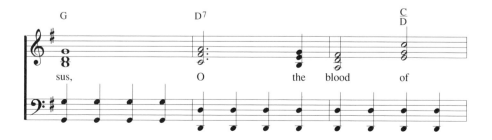

sus, O the blood of

Je - sus, O the

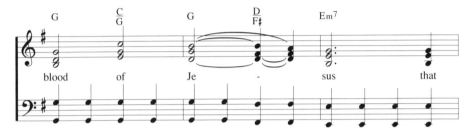

blood of Je - sus that

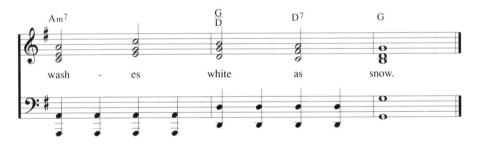

wash - es white as snow.

73

I Will Stand

Words & Music by
Cliff Downs, Joel Lindsey,
Pamela Thum & Regie Hamm

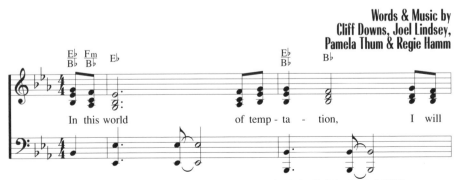

In this world of temp - ta - tion, I will

stand_____ for what is right. With a heart of sal-

va - tion, I will hold_____ up the light. If I

live or if__ I die,_____ if I laugh or if__ I cry,

In this world of temp - ta - tion, I will

stand.

74   I'm Yours

Words & Music by
Gary Chapman

CHORUS

I'm Yours, Lord; ev-ery-thing I've got, ev-ery-thing I
am, ev-ery-thing I'm not. I'm Yours, Lord;
try me now and see, see if I can
be com-plete-ly Yours.

1. My life and my love I
2. You put in us all de -

3rd time to Coda

75

He Will Carry You

Words & Music by
Scott Wesley Brown

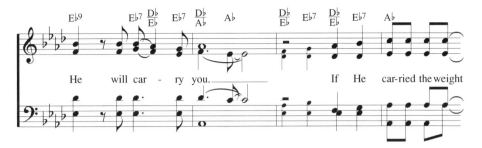

He will car - ry you._____ If He car-ried the weight

__ of the world__ up- on His shoul - der,_____ shoul - der,___

2nd time to Coda

I know, my sis - ter, that He will car - ry you._____ He said,

"Come un - to Me all who are wea - ry and

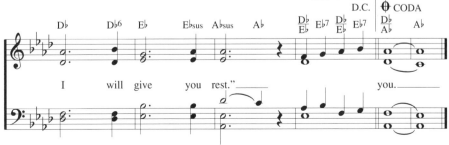

I will give you rest."_____ you._____

76
His Love Is Strong

Words & Music by
Joel Lindsey & Regie Hamm

1. So man-y moun-tains that we try to climb,
2. With-in the won-der of a ba-by's cry,

So man-y pla-ces where we fall be-hind.
And in the thun-der of a mid-night sky,

Deep in the strug-gle just to find our way,
Is some-thing strong-er than the heart of steel.

We lose the heart, we lose the faith.
It's a pow-er you can touch and feel.

Some-times this life can tear your world a-part,
So when you're think-in' all your hope is gone,

77 I Build My Life on You

Ken Bible

Randall Dennis

1. On You, O Lord,___ On You, O Lord,___ I build my life___
2. In You, O Lord,___ In You, O Lord,___ I live this day___

___ on You. You speak to me;___ I lis - ten, Lord,___ for
___ in You. You're with me now;___ I wor - ship You___ in

all that You'd have___ me do. As step by step___ You
spir - it and___ in truth. My Prince of Peace,___ Al -

lead me on,___ In faith I'll fol - low thro'.___ On You, O Lord,___
might - y God,___ With all Your love in view,___ In You, O Lord,___

My Turn Now

78

Words & Music by
Steven Curtis Chapman & Brent Lamb

79

Hosanna

Words and Music by
Cathy Jeffers Risse

Ho - san - na, ho - san - na, ho - san - na to___ the King! Ex -

alt Him and wor - ship Him— Lord of ev - 'ry - thing! Al -

might - y De - fend - er— His ban - ner goes___ be - fore. Sing your

prais - es to___ the King of Kings and Lord, the Lord of Lords.___

Al -

Lifting Up My Voice

80

Words & Music by
Dan Whittemore

Je - sus, I bow my heart be - fore___ You,

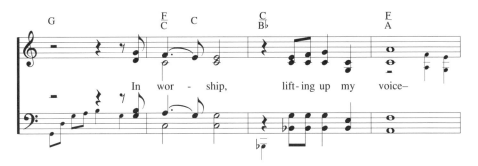

In wor - ship, lift-ing up my voice—

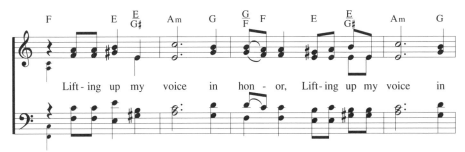

Lift-ing up my voice in hon - or, Lift-ing up my voice in

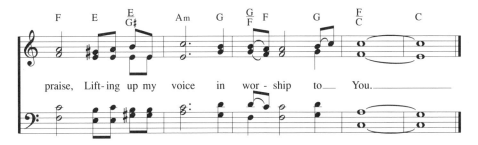

praise, Lift-ing up my voice in wor - ship to___ You.___

81 God Is in Control

Words & Music by
Twila Paris

This is— no time for fear. This is— a time for— faith— and de-
ter - mi - na - tion. Don't lose— the vi - sion here, car - ried— a -
way by e - mo - tion. Hold on— to all that— you hide in— your
heart. There is— one thing that— has al - ways— been true.
It holds the world to - geth - er.

CHORUS

God is in con-trol. We be-lieve that His chil-dren will not be for-sak-en. God is in con-trol. We will choose to re-mem-ber and nev-er be shak-en. There is no pow-er a-bove or be-side Him, we know. Oh,

God is in con-trol. Oh, God is in con-trol.

82 · King Jesus Is All

unknown
arr. by Steven V. Taylor

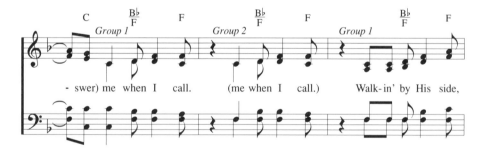

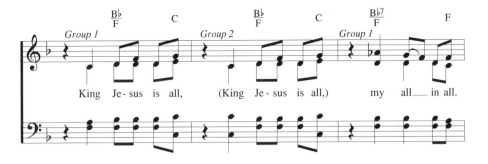

King Je - sus is all, (King Je - sus is all,) my all—— in all.

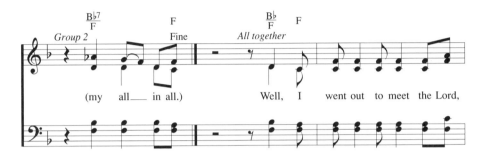

(my all—— in all.) Well, I went out to meet the Lord,

oh, yeah! I got down on—— my knees, uh, huh. I

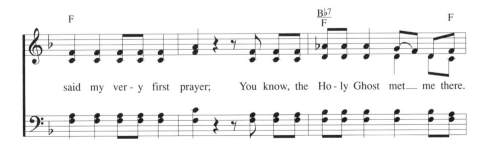

said my ver - y first prayer; You know, the Ho - ly Ghost met—— me there.

Well, I stepped on the Rock; the Rock was sound. Oh,—

— the love of God— came a - tum - blin' down. The

rea - son I know— that He saved my soul is— I

dug down deep and I found pure gold.—

D.C. al Fine

I Love You, O My Lord

83

Words & Music by
Dan Whittemore

1. I____ love You, O my____ Lord; I____ love You, O my____
2. You____ save me when I____ call; You____ save me when I____
3. Who____ keeps the lamp - light____ burn - ing? Who turns the dark a -
4. I____ love you, O my____ Lord; I____ love You, O my____

Lord,_____ My____ Rock, my Sav - ior, my De - liv - er - er—
call._____ There____ is no tri - umph for my en - e - my—
way?_____ Who____ lifts my spir - it when I sor - row?
Lord._____ O____ You are wor - thy of all prais - es—

I love You,— O my____ Lord. I love You,— O my____ Lord.

84 We Are the Light

Words & Music by
Tom McLain

Carry the Torch

85

Words & Music by
David Baroni & Lynn Keesecker

86 Hidden Treasure

Ken Bible

Randall Dennis

love with joy___ and free - dom___ He is God, and God___ with - in.
rest in His a - bun - dance, And re - joice in who___ He is.

CHORUS

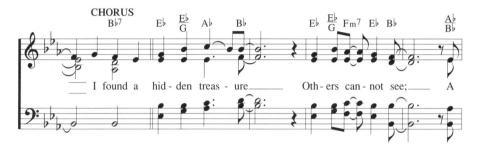

___ I found a hid - den treas - ure___ Oth - ers can - not see;___ A

hid - den treas - ure; God a - live___ in me.___ Since He

brought His king - dom in, I'm liv - ing in and un - to Him.

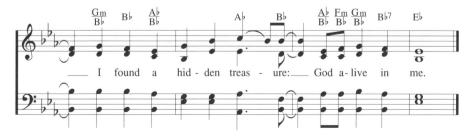

___ I found a hid - den treas - ure:___ God a - live in me.

87 Shoes

Nan Allen

Dennis Allen

1. Whenever I feel my faith is strong, it's
2. With a helmet and sword and a righteous vest, I

cause I've got my armor on. Whenever I
still don't feel I'm fully dressed. I need a shield of

feel my faith is weak, I start by lookin' down at the
faith and a belt of truth, but there's one more thing, I gotta

CHORUS

soles of my feet!
have my shoes! I need to put on my shoes, my gospel shoes,

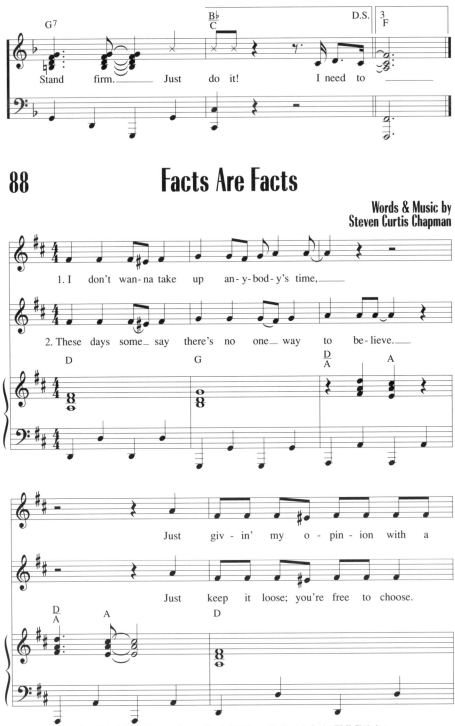

88

Facts Are Facts

Words & Music by
Steven Curtis Chapman

Stand firm.___ Just do it! I need to___

1. I don't wan-na take up an-y-bod-y's time,___

2. These days some__ say there's no one__ way to be-lieve.___

Just giv-in' my o-pin-ion with a

Just keep it loose; you're free to choose.

com - in' back, 'cause prom - is - es are prom - is - es and facts are facts!

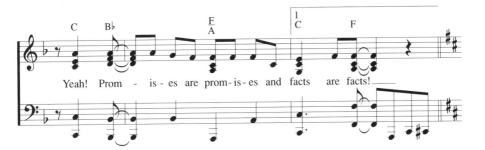

Yeah! Prom - is - es are prom-is-es and facts are facts!

facts are facts! And I___ be- lieve Je- sus, He's com- in' back! I

___ know there's a God who knows___ my name___ and a Son___ who___

died   to   take   the blame.   I___   be - lieve   Je - sus   is

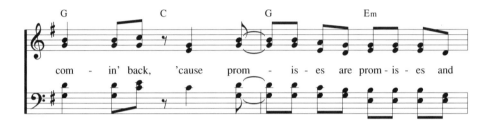

com - in' back,   'cause   prom   -   is - es   are prom - is - es   and

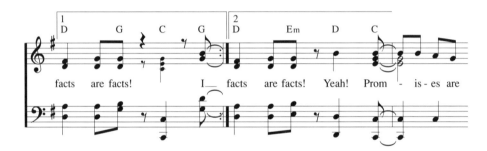

facts   are facts!   I___ facts   are facts!   Yeah!   Prom   -   is - es   are

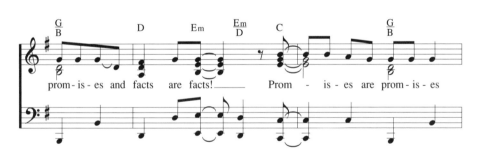

prom - is - es and facts   are facts!___   Prom   -   is - es   are prom - is - es

and facts   are facts!

Ken Bible

Stephen V. Taylor

90   Leaning on the Everlasting Arms

Elisha Hoffman

Anthony Showalter
arr. by Dennis Allen

CHORUS

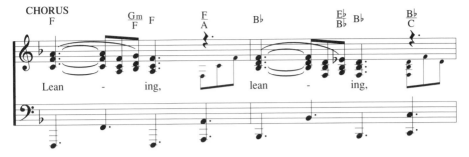

Lean - ing, lean - ing,

safe and se - cure from all a - larms,

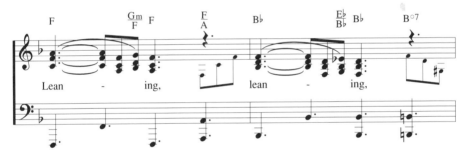

Lean - ing, lean - ing,

lean - ing on the ev - er - last - ing

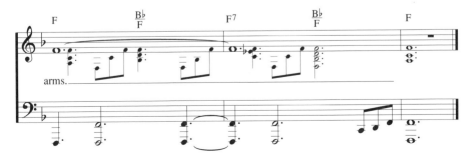

arms.

91   Great Is the Lord

Words and Music by
Patrick Henderson

Great is_ the Lord;_____ He is great to__ be praised_____ in the

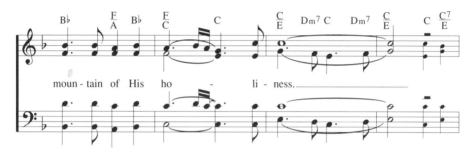

moun - tain of His ho - li - ness._____

Great is__ the Lord;_____ He is great to__ be praised_____ in the

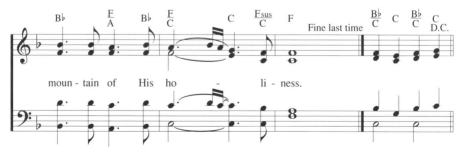

moun - tain of His ho - li - ness.

Clap Your Hands

92

Words & Music by
Danny Hamilton

Clap your hands all ye peo-ple. Shout it to the Lord with the voice tri-um-phant. Clap your hands, clap your hands. Praise Him with the sound of the voice and trum-pet. Clap your hands, clap your hands. Shout it from the top of the tall-est moun-tain. Clap your hands, clap your hands and praise the Lord.

93
Higher Ground

Johnson Oatman, Jr.

Dennis Allen

1. I'm press-ing on____ the up - ward way;____
2. I want to live____ a - bove the world,____

All (or Group 2)

1. I'm press - ing on____ the
2. I want to live____ a -

New heights I'm gain - ing ev - ery day.
Tho' Sa - tan's darts____ at me are hurled.

up - ward way;____ New
bove the world,____ Tho'

Seek Ye First

94

Words & Music by
Karen Lafferty

Above All Else

Words & Music by
Kirk & Deby Dearman

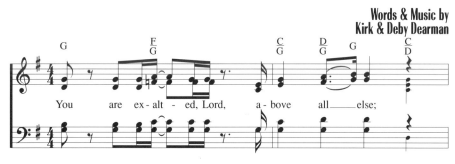

You are ex - alt - ed, Lord, a - bove all____ else;

We place You at the high - est place a - bove all____ else.

Right now where we stand___ and ev - ery - where we___ go,

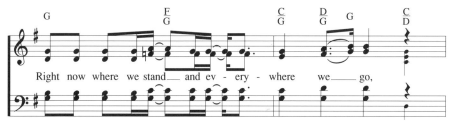

We place You at the high - est place so the world will know:

You are a Might - y War - rior dressed in ar - mor of light,

Crush-ing the deeds of dark - ness, lead us on__ in the fight.

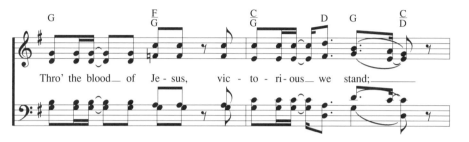

Thro' the blood__ of Je - sus, vic - to - ri - ous__ we stand;____

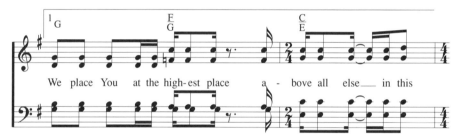

We place You at the high-est place a - bove all else__ in this

land._____ We place You at the high-est place a -

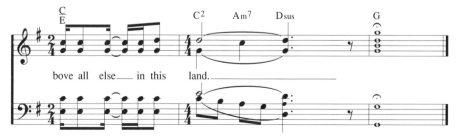

bove all else__ in this land._____

96 Thy Word

Words & Music by
Amy Grant & Michael W. Smith

Thy Word is a lamp un-to my feet___ and a light un-to my path.

path.

Thy Word is a lamp un-to my feet___ and a light un-to my path.

path. path. Thy Word is a lamp un-to my feet___ and a light un-to my path.

Joy!

George W. Cook

Amy Grant

1, 3. I got the joy, (joy) joy, (joy) joy, (joy) I got the joy, (joy) joy, (joy) joy, (joy) I got the joy, (joy) joy, (joy) joy,

2. I got the love, (love) love, (love), love, (love) I got the love, (love) love, (love), love, (love) I got the love, (love) love, (love)

(Shout) *Two, three, four!* Down in my heart, down in my heart, down in my heart to stay, down in my heart to stay!

(Clap) (Clap)

98   I Will Call upon the Lord

Adapted by Michael O'Shields

Michael O'Shields

Lord_____ liv-eth, and bless-ed be the Rock, And let the God___

_____ of my sal-va-tion be ex - alt - ed. The Lord_____ liv-eth, and

bless-ed be the Rock, And let the God___ of my sal-va-tion be ex-

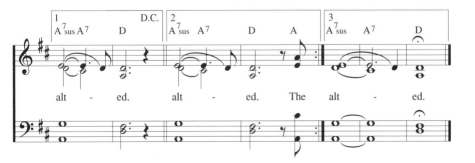

alt - ed.   alt - ed. The   alt - ed.

99   **Build a Bridge**

Words & Music by
Dennis & Nan Allen

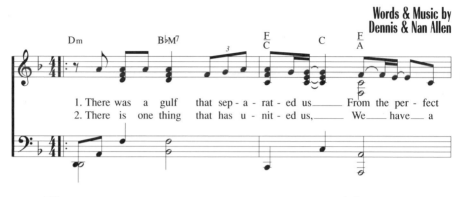

1. There was a gulf that sep-a-rat-ed us____ From the per-fect
2. There is one thing that has u-nit-ed us,____ We____ have____ a

heart of____God.____ But with the gift of His____own
bond of____faith.____ And to-geth-er we____can

Son, God made the way for us____ to cross.
build a bridge His love thro' us____ cre-ates.

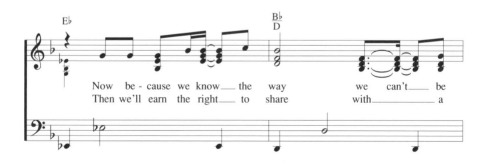

Now be-cause we know____the way we can't be
Then we'll earn the right____to share with____a

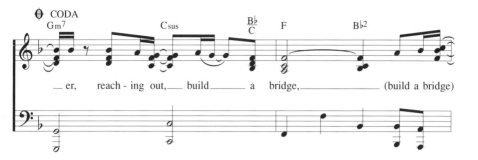

CODA

er, reach-ing out,— build a bridge,— (build a bridge)

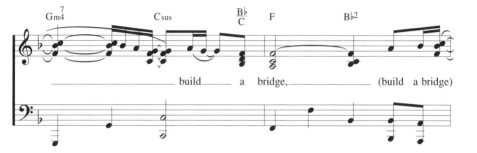

build a bridge,— (build a bridge)

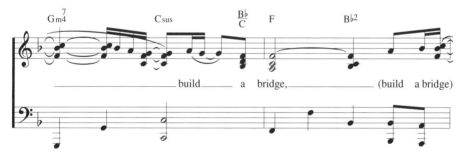

build a bridge,— (build a bridge)

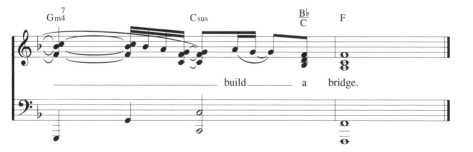

build a bridge.

TOPICAL INDEX

ALPHABETICAL INDEX